Manufactured by Amazon.ca
Bolton, ON

15947458R00057